Xiuhtezcatl Martinez
Protecting the Environment and Indigenous Rights

Linda Barghoorn

Crabtree Publishing Company

www.crabtreebooks.com

Author: Linda Barghoorn

Series research and development: Reagan Miller

Editorial director: Kathy Middleton

Editor: Crystal Sikkens

Proofreader: Wendy Scavuzzo

Photo researchers: Samara Parent and Crystal Sikkens

Designer and prepress technician: Samara Parent

Print coordinator: Margaret Amy Salter

Photographs:

Earthguardians.org: title page, pages 6, 10-11, 12-13, 14-15, 16, 17, 20, 23, 26, 28, 30

Getty Images: © Barry King: cover; © Helen H. Richardson: pages 4-5; © Paul Zimmerman: pages 7, 29; © Frazer Harrison: page 9; © Charley Gallay: page 18; © Michael Stewart: pages 19, 22; © CARL DE SOUZA: page 21; © ANTONIO SCORZA: page 27

All other images from Shutterstock

About the author: Linda Barghoorn grew up in Fonthill, Ontario and attended Brock University in St. Catharines, where she graduated with a Bachelor of Arts in German. She spent twenty years living outside Canada – in Europe and the Middle East – during which time she began writing about and photographing her experiences. She is married with two grown daughters, and lives and works in Toronto, Canada.

Library and Archives Canada Cataloguing in Publication

Barghoorn, Linda, author
    Xiuhtezcatl Martinez : protecting the environment and indigenous rights / Linda Barghoorn.

(Remarkable lives revealed)
Includes index.
Issued in print and electronic formats.
ISBN 978-0-7787-3421-5 (hardback).—
ISBN 978-0-7787-3425-3 (paperback).--
ISBN 978-1-4271-1920-9 (html)

    1. Martinez, Xiuhtezcatl--Juvenile literature. 2. Environmentalists--United States--Biography--Juvenile literature. 3. Environmentalism--Juvenile literature. 4. Human rights workers--United States--Biography--Juvenile literature. 5. Indians of North America--Civil rights--Juvenile literature. 6. Rap musicians--United States--Biography--Juvenile literature. I. Title.

GE195.5.B368 2017   j333.72092   C2016-907103-0
                                                            C2016-907104-9

Library of Congress Cataloging-in-Publication Data

Names: Barghoorn, Linda, author.
Title: Xiuhtezcatl Martinez : protecting the environment and Indigenous rights / Linda Barghoorn.
Description: New York, New York : Crabtree Publishing Company, 2017. | Series: Remarkable lives revealed | Includes index.
Identifiers: LCCN 2016048893 (print) | LCCN 2016051811 (ebook) | ISBN 9780778734215 (reinforced library binding : alkaline paper) | ISBN 9780778734253 (paperback : alkaline paper) | ISBN 9781427119209 (Electronic HTML)
Subjects: LCSH: Martinez, Xiuhtezcatl--Juvenile literature. | Environmentalists--United States--Biography--Juvenile literature. | Climatic changes--Juvenile literature. | Political activists--United States--Biography--Juvenile literature. | Indigenous peoples--Civil rights--Juvenile literature. | Aztecs--Biography--Juvenile literature. | Teenagers--United States--Biography--Juvenile literature. | Musicians--United States--Biography--Juvenile literature. | Hip-hop--Juvenile literature.
Classification: LCC GE56.M334 B37 2017 (print) | LCC GE56.M334 (ebook) | DDC 363.70092 [B] --dc23
LC record available at https://lccn.loc.gov/2016048893

Crabtree Publishing Company
www.crabtreebooks.com   1-800-387-7650

Printed in Canada/022017/CH20161214

Published in Canada
Crabtree Publishing
616 Welland Ave.
St. Catharines, Ontario
L2M 5V6

Published inthe United States
Crabtree Publishing
PMB 59051
350 Fifth Ave., 59th Floor
New York, NY 10118

Published in theUnited Kingdom
Crabtree Publishing
Maritime House
Basin Road North, Hove
BN41 1WR

Published in Australia
Crabtree Publishing
3 Charles Street
Coburg North
VIC, 3058

Contents

Xiuhtezcatl Martinez

Everyone's lives are made up of many experiences and stories. Some life stories, known as biographies, may be remarkable or inspiring to others. Everyone has a different idea of what makes someone remarkable. Xiuhtezcatl (Shu-TEZ-caht) Tonatiuh (Toh-NAH-tee-yoo) Martinez (Mar-TEEN-ehz) is considered a remarkable person by many. His passion and determination to create a healthier, more **sustainable** planet has made him a superstar of the youth-led **climate change** movement. A movement is created when a large group of people join together to change the way we think or act.

What Is a Biography?

A biography is the story of a person's life. We read biographies to learn about a person's experiences and thoughts. Biographies can be based on many sources of information. Primary sources include a person's own words or pictures. Secondary sources included friends, family, media, and research.

Climate Warrior

Xiuhtezcatl has been on the frontlines of environmental issues since he was six years old. He has worked tirelessly to raise awareness about Earth's destruction. He speaks with authority and confidence as he encourages his generation to step forward as leaders and use their passions to write new rules for the kind of world they want to live in. As you read his story, think about why many people find Xiuhtezcatl remarkable.

? THINK ABOUT IT

Do you know someone remarkable? What qualities do they have that you admire?

Xiuhtezcatl feels a strong connection to the beauty of Colorado, where he grew up.

Aztec Roots and Activism

Xiuhtezcatl was born in Boulder, Colorado, in 2000. His father Siri (SIH-ree) Martinez is of Aztec descent. His mother Tamara Roske (RAW-skee) is American. His name was given to him by his Aztec **elders**, based on the position of the stars when he was born. It comes from the Nahuatl (Nah-WHA-tel), or Aztec, language. Like the Mashika (Mah-SHEE-kah) people, with whom he shares his heritage, Xiuhtezcatl feels a strong connection to Earth. As **indigenous** people, they were the original **guardians** of the land.

Aztecs

The Aztecs are descendants of the Mashika, a nomadic tribe from northern Mexico who settled in the valley of Mexico.

Xiuhtezcatl takes part in a cultural ceremony celebrating his Aztec roots.

A Family of Activists

Xiuhtezcatl inherited his deep commitment to **activism** from his family. His father taught him about his culture's respect for Earth. They spent much of his childhood exploring nature together. His mother is an environmental activist. She created the Earth Guardians organization to inspire young people to lead a climate change movement. Xiuhtezcatl's sisters and brother use music to help communicate their message of concern about the environment and to encourage others to get involved.

? THINK ABOUT IT

How did Xiuhtezcatl's heritage influence his concern for the planet?

Xiuhtezcatl and his younger brother Itzcuauhtli (eet-SKWAT-lee) work closely together to raise awareness about climate change.

Protecting Our Planet

Xiuhtezcatl believes that climate change is the most important issue of his generation. As a child, he realized that the world he loved was being destroyed. He believes the way we think about Earth—that it belongs to us and can be **exploited** until there is nothing left—has been inherited from past generations. They cut down forests, mined for oil, and polluted the air without considering the future. He wants young people to reconnect with Earth, to nurture and protect it.

Deforestation happens when large areas of trees are cut down. The wood is used for many things such as building houses and making paper.

Philosophy for Change

Many adults believe that young people lack the knowledge and skills to be effective leaders. But Xiuhtezcatl is challenging that **stereotype**. He believes his generation has the skills, creativity, and dedication to lead a movement for change. He encourages youth to use their art, poetry, and music to bring attention to climate change issues and communicate with each other. He is not afraid to confront traditional ideas of what we think is possible—or impossible—as he pushes governments and industry leaders for better laws to protect Earth.

> " There is a movement on the rise and our generation is on the front of that movement. "
>
> —**Xiuhtezcatl Martinez, United Nations General Assembly on Climate Change, 2015**

Xiuhtezcatl speaks at a WE Day celebration in California, where young activists get together to celebrate their accomplishments and inspire others.

Earth Guardians

Xiuhtezcatl carries on the work of the Earth Guardians organization that his mother started in 1995. Earth Guardians is a tribe of young activists, artists, and musicians from around the world. They have stepped forward as leaders to create their unique vision for a healthier, more sustainable future. Instead of waiting for global leaders to act, they are channeling their energy and enthusiasm to demand that urgent climate issues be addressed NOW. Together, they demonstrate the shared power of their generation to make big things happen.

RYSE

As its youth director, Xiuhtezcatl is the driving force behind Earth Guardians. He leads a group called RYSE: Rising Youth for a Sustainable Earth. With Xiuhtezcatl's leadership, young people are stepping forward to participate in and lead environmental discussions and campaigns around the world. He is encouraging young people to challenge the way things have usually been done by industry and government leaders. Until now, these actions have done little to fix the climate change problem. Xiuhtezcatl wants to see real change to help save the planet before it's too late.

EARTH GUARDIANS
Youth for Global Su
w.EarthGuardians

Xiuhtezcatl has led people of all ages who've joined in marches and protests around the world to fight against climate change.

Youth Council

RYSE's youth council consists of 18 young leaders from across North America. They have been chosen by Xiuhtezcatl for their passion, enthusiasm, and creativity. Their goal is to build a global network of activists by training and encouraging others to join their movement. The council also develops climate action plans to help protect the environment in their own neighborhoods and around the world.

*As a youth council member, Xiuhtezcatl has led local projects to forbid **pesticide** use in parks, initiate a fee for plastic grocery bags, and ban **fracking** in his home state of Colorado.*

Wisdom Council

RYSE also has a wisdom council of elders, made up of activists, writers, artists, and environmentalists. The elders come from many different cultural backgrounds and age groups. They provide unique perspectives and knowledge that they have gathered throughout their life. The youth and wisdom councils work as partners to train youth leaders around the world. They also work together to create climate action plans.

? THINK ABOUT IT

What skills or qualities do members of the youth and wisdom councils contribute?

Source of All Wisdom

In many indigenous cultures, elders are considered the source of all wisdom. Younger tribe members respect their age, wisdom, and experience.

Climate Action Plans

Each season, Earth Guardians around the world put the climate action plans to work. Crews in each country decide what kind of project best serves their community. Projects have included wells for water in Africa, clean up of parks and beaches in the United States, and tree-planting in Bhutan. In India, crews spoke with drivers to raise awareness about air pollution. In Brazil, they staged a concert to highlight the importance of protecting water resources. Xiuhtezcatl and his youth council help promote these events to encourage others to get involved.

Speakers Bureau

The speakers bureau is a small team of youth leaders who are the voice of Earth Guardians. They speak at conferences, school assemblies, protest marches, and media events. Stories of their personal work on projects such as deforestation, indigenous rights, and green entrepreneurship help to inspire others. As a member of the speakers bureau, Xiuhtezcatl has participated in more than 100 events around the world to raise environmental awareness and action.

Green Entrepreneurship

Green entrepreneurship is the ability to create a new brand of business using renewable or recycling strategies.

Teams from Earth Guardians have planted trees in more than twenty countries around the world.

The Change-Maker

Xiuhtezcatl has always loved music. He plays piano, writes music, and can rap in English and Spanish. He looks forward to the day when he can dedicate himself fully to a career as a musician. Until then, he is using his music as an instrument in his role as an activist. In 2012, his music was used in a documentary called "Trust Colorado" which received the Best Environmental Film Documentary award.

Music breaks down barriers. Music is what connects people.

—Xiuhtezcatl Martinez, Upworthy.com, Dec 2015

Xiuhtezcatl uses rap music to help educate young people about environmental issues.

Eco Hip-Hop Artist

Xiuhtezcatl describes himself as an **eco** hip-hop artist and activist. He often performs with and his younger brother Itzcuauhtli and his three sisters, Isa Caress, Tonantzin (Toe-NAHN-sine), and Jasmine. They have performed at United Nations **summits**, schools, conferences, and music festivals around the world. They have recorded two albums called *Journey* and *Generation RYSE*. Their songs deal with many different issues. "What the Frack" protests against the practice of fracking for oil. "Speak for the Trees" is a plea to help save our forests.

United Nations

The United Nations is a government organization with representatives from almost 200 countries who work to promote cooperation on global issues.

Xiuhtezcatl's family of musicians and activists is helping to change the world with songs that have a powerful message about the environment.

Traveling the World

Xiuhtezcatl spends much of the year traveling and is regularly at the center of political and environmental events. In 2015, he was selected to join a National Geographic expedition to the Arctic to study glaciers, which are melting due to climate change. On Earth Day 2016, he attended the United Nations' historic signing of a global climate **pact** to reduce levels of harmful **greenhouse gases**. While there, he finally met Leonardo DiCaprio, whose movie about global warming, called *The 11th Hour,* launched Xiuhtezcatl's career into activism when he was six years old.

Leonardo DiCaprio's movie, The 11th Hour, *features science experts who explore the impact of humans on planet Earth and what we can do to change.*

Too Young to Vote

During the 2016 U.S. presidential campaign, Xiuhtezcatl made an online plea to U.S. presidential candidates Hillary Clinton and Donald Trump. He urged them to consider the climate change priorities of 74 million youth under eighteen—like Xiuhtezcatl—who can't vote. Although he did not have a voice in the election, Xiuhtezcatl spoke out to insist that the next president must take climate change seriously and take action to address it.

> We are not going to sit idly by while governments and presidents make decisions for us.
>
> **—Xiuhtezcatl Martinez, TedX Youth@ Mile High, 2014**

Xiuhtezcatl joined global leaders and activists at the Social Good Summit to discuss how technology and media can help solve some of the planet's greatest challenges.

Climate Lawsuit

Xiuhtezcatl is frustrated by the government's lack of action to tackle the urgent issue of climate change. In August 2015, he was part of a group of 21 young people who filed a historic **lawsuit** against the U.S. government. It is viewed as the most important lawsuit on the planet. It claims the government has known about the dangers of climate change for years, but has done almost nothing about it. Xiuhtezcatl's group believes that everyone has the right to live on a healthy planet with access to healthy air, water, and land. The lawsuit blames the government for not protecting this right. They want the government to reduce the use of **fossil fuels**, which pollute the atmosphere.

The 2014 People's Climate Change March was the largest in history, with more than 400,000 people attending in New York City.

Science Versus Industry

Dr. James Hansen is one of the world's leading climate scientists. He submitted a statement in support of the lawsuit. But, the government and fossil-fuel industry strongly oppose the lawsuit. They suggest that it would create impossible restrictions on how companies do business. Xiuhtezcatl argues that they are putting their desire to make money ahead of the planet's well-being. He wants companies to create business plans and strategies that will address climate-change issues.

? THINK ABOUT IT

What does the lawsuit fight for?

Climate Change

Dr. Hansen was the first to bring climate change to the public's attention in 1988.

CLIMATE CHANGE

A MATTER OF LIFE OR DEATH

Dr. Hansen believes we must all take part in the fight against climate change if we want to preserve life on Earth.

Saving Planet Earth

Xiuhtezcatl believes our modern lifestyles are too disconnected from the planet. We don't often think about how our daily behavior affects the planet we call home. We are destroying Earth without thinking about it. But, we cannot simply move to another planet if we are no longer able to live on Earth. We need to reduce our carbon footprint to create a more sustainable world for everyone to enjoy. Each of us has a role to play in this. Small individual steps can create big changes.

Carbon Footprint

A carbon footprint measures the environmental impact of a person's lifestyle in units of carbon dioxide.

The Social Good Summit unites people in a global discussion about how to create a more sustainable world.

Could You Be an Earth Guardian?

Are you willing to help create the change that Xiuhtezcatl is fighting for? Here are some principles to guide you as an Earth Guardian:

- **Put Earth first in all your actions.**
- **Never accept the phrase "it's impossible."**
- **Collaborate with others to develop positive and powerful team relationships.**
- **Be ready to help lead, and to support and inspire other leaders.**
- **Stop talking and start DOING.**

Earth Guardians are passionate, energetic, and optimistic in their belief that we CAN change the world.

Simple Ways to Save Earth

There are many simple actions that each of us can do to help reduce our carbon footprint and work toward a healthier and sustainable Earth. For many of us, the first step is to become more aware of how our actions affect our planet. It's important to educate ourselves. Then we can make informed decisions that will guide our actions to make Earth a better place to live.

Fossil fuels such as coal are burned to provide energy for factories. We need to find new ways to create energy that do not pollute our atmosphere.

> *The biggest challenge we face is shifting human **consciousness**.*
>
> **—Xiuhtezcatl Martinez, Eco-Watch, April 2015**

Action Checklist

✓ **Turn off the lights** when you leave a room.

✓ **Turn off the water** while shampooing your hair or brushing your teeth.

✓ **Avoid buying bottled water**; use a reusable water bottle instead.

✓ **Compost** leftover food instead of throwing it in the trash.

✓ **Walk, ride a bike, or take public transit** instead of using the family car.

✓ **Pick up litter** when you walk.

✓ **Plant trees** in your neighborhood.

✓ **Organize a neighborhood cleanup.**

✓ **Recycle** whenever possible.

✓ **Use rechargeable batteries** instead of disposable batteries.

? THINK ABOUT IT

Can you think of other actions to add to the checklist?

Teenage Achievements

Since becoming an environmentalist and activist, Xiuhtezcatl has created an enormous movement, with 2,000 crews of young people across five continents. He has taken part in more than 100 rallies and protests, and worked with 50 environmental organizations across the globe. He vows to continue his work as an activist until his generation's future on Earth is safe and secure.

> "Together we can change the world. We owe it to future generations to be the leaders of today.
>
> —Xiuhtezcatl Martinez, United Nations General Assembly on Climate Change, 2015

In 2013, he was one of 24 youth **change-makers** selected to the President's Youth Council. This council shares their ideas for policies that will shape the country's future.

Global Influence

Xiuhtezcatl's influence spans the globe—from teenagers to celebrities and world leaders. Although still only a teenager himself, he has spoken to country leaders and representatives at the United Nations (UN) three times! He was the youngest speaker at the UN's 2012 Earth Summit in Brazil, where he also had the honor of joining indigenous elders to light the sacred fire.

Sacred Fire Ceremony

A sacred fire ceremony is a traditional ritual in which indigenous tribe members gather around a fire. Tribe members promise to abandon negative ideas and to embrace new beginnings.

Xiuhtezcatl participates in a Sacred Fire Ceremony at the indigenous village of Kari-Oca during the UN 2012 Summit.

Awards

Xiuhtezcatl's work has been honored with many awards. In 2013, President Obama presented him with the President's Volunteer Service Award. This award recognizes American citizens who have dedicated themselves to volunteer activities. It honors them for setting a high standard of service, and inspiring others to do the same. In 2015, Xiuhtezcatl was one of five youth winners of a $25,000 prize from Peace First, who recognized his passion and courage to inspire change. Peace First is a national organization dedicated to creating the next generation of peacemakers.

The Face of Change

Xiuhtezcatl is a celebrity teenage activist. His work has been highlighted on PBS, National Geographic, and HBO networks. In 2013, HDNet TV broadcast a special Earth Day program featuring Xiuhtezcatl's and Itzcuauhtli's work as Earth Guardians. Xiuhtezcatl was the subject of a 2015 documentary by film-maker Vanessa Black, called *Kid Warrior: The Xiuhtezcatl Martinez Story*. He was also featured in a documentary television series, called *Years of Living Dangerously*, which focused on global warming. Xiuhtezcatl Martinez is truly the face of change as he works to create a generation of change-makers.

Xiuhtezcatl and Itzcuauhtli attend the premiere of Saving My Tomorrow, *a documentary film in which children share their thoughts on taking care of our planet.*

Writing Prompts

1. Are you inspired by Xiuhtezcatl's work? What impresses you the most about what he is doing?

2. Do you believe his youth movement has the power to help make the world a better place? Why?

3. Do you feel the lawsuit Xiuhtezcatl has brought against the United States government is an effective way to fight climate change? Why?

4. Discuss some of the ways you can be involved in making positive changes for the environment.

Learning More

Books

Everything Kids' Environment Book by Sheri Amsel. Adams Media, 2007.

A Hot Planet Needs Cool Kids: Understanding Climate Change and What You Can Do About It by Julie Hall. Greenleaf Book Group, 2007.

A Kids' Guide to Climate Change and Global Warming by Cathryn Berger Kaye. Free Spirit Publishing, 2009.

Your Local Environment by Sally Hewitt. Crabtree Publishing Company, 2009.

Human Footprint: Everything You Will Eat, Use, Wear, Buy, and Throw Out in Your Lifetime by Ellen Kirk. National Geographic Kids, 2011.

The New 50 Simple Things Kids Can Do to Save the Earth by The EarthWorks Group. Andrews McMeel Publishing, 2009.

Websites

www.earthguardians.org
Outlines work being done by the Earth Guardians organization and encourages readers to get involved.

http://sparkaction.org/changemaker/youth-changemaker-xiuhtezcatl-martinez
Profiles the young life and accomplishments of Xiuhtezcatl, including a short documentary video.

www.cgrising.com/heroines-gallery/xiuhtezcatl-martinez
Highlights Xiuhtezcatl and his work, with links to Earth Guardians website, Earth Guardians' page on YouTube, Facebook, and news updates.

https://ecokids.ca/take-action
Offers online activities and games to inspire children to become environmental guardians.

www.xiuhtezcatl.com
Extensive website outlining Xiuhtezcatl's life, work, awards, videos, photos, and more.

Glossary

activism The practice of using strong actions to support big changes in society

change-maker Someone who leads change in society

compost To recycle decayed food into a mixture that can improve soil in a garden

consciousness A person's awareness of an issue

climate change The process in which the environment changes to become warmer, colder, drier, or wetter than normal. This can occur naturally, or it can be caused by human activity.

deforestation The act of cutting down all the trees in an area

eco Slang for "ecological"; environmental

elder A person who has authority because of their age or experience

exploit To use something in a way that is unfair and that does damage to it

fossil fuel A fuel such as coal, oil, or natural gas that is formed in the earth over millions of years from dead plants or animals

fracking A method of drilling into the earth and injecting water, sand, and chemicals to separate oil or gas from the rock

greenhouse gases The gases in Earth's atmosphere, such as carbon dioxide, that contribute to the warming of the planet

guardian Someone that watches over or protects something

indigenous Describing someone or something that is native to the land they are living on

lawsuit A legal challenge in court to end a disagreement

nomadic Describing a group of people who move from place to place

pact A formal agreement between people, groups, or countries

pesticide A chemical used to kill insects that damages plants or crops

stereotype An unfair or untrue belief about a group of people

summit A meeting between government leaders of different countries

sustainable Something that can be used without being finished up or destroyed

Index